AUSTRALIA

DOUGLASS BAGLIN * YVONNE AUSTIN

NationaL

Published by National Book Distributors
19A Roger Street,
Brookvale, NSW, 2100

First edition 1978
Second edition 1980
Third edition 1982
Reprinted 1983
Fourth edition 1984
Fifth edition 1987
Reprinted 1988 (twice)
Reprinted 1991
Reprinted 1993
© Douglas Baglin and Yvonne Austin
    1978, 1980, 1982, 1984, 1987

Typeset in Australia by Deblaere Typesetting Pty Ltd
Printed in Hong Kong by Everbest Printing Co. Ltd

National Library of Australia
Cataloguing-in-Publication data

Baglin, Douglas, 1926–
    Australia.

ISBN 1 875580 13 1.

1. Australia — Description and travel — 1976–1990.
Views. I. Austin, Yvonne. II. Title.

994.0630222

All rights reserved. Subject to the Copyright Act 1968, no part of this publication may be reproduced, stored in a retrieval system, or transmitted in any form, or by any means, electronic, mechanical, photocopying, recording, or otherwise, without the prior written permission of the publisher.

AUSTRALIA

Australia is many things to many people, infinite in variety and splendour, beautiful, harsh and uncompromising. It is a patient land, vast, full of contrasts, and totally unpredictable.

Australia is unique in being the smallest most sparsely populated continent and the world's largest island. Its massive size, location and landforms govern the climate which varies to extremes. Nearly 40 percent of the land mass lies north of the Tropic of Capricorn, while to the south-east are extensive non-permanent snowfields. The vegetation is varied and spectacular, ranging from isolated tufts of ephemerals to lush tropical jungles.

Water is the key to Australia's character, with flood and drought between them laying down the terms that mean destruction or survival, offering supreme challenges to man's endurance and will to remain and wage battle

A close encounter of the bird kind, Wauchope, New South Wales.

More and more women are entering what had been only considered an exclusively male domain. This young lady sheep shearer doesn't seem to find it a too-daunting task.

against these relentless elements. Over one third of the country's seven and a half million square kilometres receives about 250mm of rain each year, while the eastern coast receives substantial rainfall, varying from area to area. Towards the arid centre the rainfall diminishes dramatically.

The two major wind systems, the south-east trades and light westerlies, extend over different areas in summer and winter. Because of this the north of the continent receives its 'wet' season from the summer north-west monsoons, and its 'dry' in winter, while the south receives the majority of its rainfall in winter. The centre is usually heated and dried by both wind systems, and rarely wet by either.

In many areas the rainfall is erratic. Some places experience their whole supply in one downfall. In other regions the rain is predictable and regular, but drought invariably occurs at some stage. With no water to promote new growth, the bare countryside takes on a parched tragic aspect. Creeks and waterholes dry up, and the bleached bones of animals bear mute testimony to the fierceness of this recurring blight.

Irrigation schemes have resulted in waste lands being turned into vast stretches of fertile growth. In the Murray River Valley alone, 20,000 hectares of land was converted from unproductive semi-arid waste to a wealthy highly productive fruit-growing region which has attracted thousands of people to the district.

As a transporter, water is the medium for constant change. With it, the country prospers; without enough over a regular growing season the result is drought and desert.

Most of Australia's deserts and semi-arid regions lie on the great western plateau or the lowlands of the centre. These comprise most of Western Australia and Northern Territory, the northern section of South Australia, a north-south strip occupying the western half of Queensland and New South Wales, and north-west Victoria. This huge area differs in characteristics, landforms, vegetation and fauna, and although it is generally fringed by pockets of rich fertile land, it experiences a low rainfall, high day temperatures, extensive prevailing winds and an ever-changing kaleidoscope of colours.

Salt lakes appear as a common feature of these areas. These white-crusted depressions act as basins after rain. The water passing over the hard unporous ground dissolves salts and drains into lakes. Unable to escape into the ground, and exposed to constantly high temperatures and winds, the water is soon evaporated, leaving the strange looking pock-marked depression around which a few lonely trees may live. One of the largest of these is Lake Eyre. Its total length is about 240 kilometres and it

Vast, flat, featureless country, where cattle stations are measured in square kilometres and fresh water is a precious commodity. Brunette Downs, on the Barkly Tableland in the Northern Territory, is covered by an enormous limestone shelf whose porous nature swallows surface water. This becomes trapped by a floor of cretacious shale and is made available to cattle by sub-artesian and artesian bores. Note the cattle train used to transport stock.

The snowfields of the Southern Alps, dominated by Mount Kosciusko, which, at 2228 metres, is Australia's highest peak, attracts visitors from far and wide.

covers an area of approximately 8000 square kilometres. Thousands of these lakes dot the flat arid country, but rivers are few. Those that exist are generally dry watercourses which fill from all points after the 'wet' and meander across a scorched and thirsty land before drying up altogether.

Contrasting with the dry white salt lakes are the continually drifting sand dunes. At intervals from 300 metres to two kilometres, they often rise to 70 metres and extend in length up to 300 kilometres. Indicating the direction of the prevailing winds, the dunes vary in colour from bright yellow to vivid red, and are sparsely covered with spinifex grass, mitchell grass, bluebush and saltbush.

Many of Australia's deserts are gibber plains —

The koala, a national symbol of Australia, is becoming increasingly hard to find in the wild. Living mainly on a variety of eucalypt they seldom come down from the tree tops and are best seen in sanctuaries.

millions of hot stones and rocks and windblown material covering the flat red hard-baked crust. Bleak and shadeless and hot, they have claimed the lives of brave men and fools alike. Dry creek beds, sometimes marked by river red gums, coolibahs or acacias, have soaks about a metre underground. By digging, one generally finds water. If rain comes, the landscape changes once again.

On the low sandy deserts a blue haze highlights the isolated hills and plateaux which stand naked above the flat, otherwise featureless land. In these basically flat or undulating areas, scattered outcrops of stone often emerge as huge mesas or monoliths rising sheer from the plains. Three of these, Ayers Rock, the Olgas and Mount Conner, rise within sight of each other. Situated south of Lake Amadeus, a 145-kilometre long salt pan, the Olgas are comprised of a circle of 30 huge rounded domes which rise vertically 500 metres above their surrounds and cover an area of about 65 square kilometres. Forty kilometres to their east, on the same flat trough, squats Ayers Rock, the rounded dome of a buried hill. A further 80 kilometres east, rising in sheer vertical cliffs, is the long flat-topped mesa of Mount Conner.

To the south of these three giant tors, on the South Australia-Northern Territory border, the Musgrave

The Birdsville Track, once used by drovers as a stock route, is a flat, remote, dangerous and often impassable 'road' which extends from Birdsville in south-west Queensland to Marree, South Australia, a distance of approximately 5000 kilometres. The area is arid, with temperatures hot during the day and cold at night. Surface water is scarce and with the intense heat, dust storms and sudden floods, many ill-equipped travellers have come to grief along its stretch.

Ranges climb 1000 metres from the sandy plains. Running parallel with these, and separated by the Amadeus Trough, lies another highland belt — the MacDonnell Ranges. The 400-kilometre long folded range of sedimentary rocks run in an east-west direction, a series of parallel ridges gouged by spectacular chasms and gaps. Isolated palm-fringed oases such as Palm Valley on the Finke River appear in various parts of the deserts. In these dry uninhabited regions are wealthy deposits of oil and minerals, but isolation and harsh conditions makes mining an expensive and often uneconomic proposition. The cattle industry in such areas is a gamble — some years fortunes are made; at other times stock perish.

A vast area of the arid and semi-arid regions sit on a bed of water. Huge underground lakes resting on shale lie under a cover of thick limestone. The Barkly Tableland, in north-east Northern Territory, and the Nuliarbor Plain, extending from South Australia into Western Australia,

The sulphur-crested cockatoo, is widely spread in the timbered regions of northern and eastern Australia.

The historic house, Craigend, in the Sydney suburb of Darling Point.

An uncomplicated life-style in Derby, Western Australia.

A row of terrace houses in Fremantle, Western Australia. Note the carved sandstone heads and the bargeboards framing the little figures standing in their niches.

are both riverless deserts sitting above water beds. The porous limestone simply drains any surface water into its huge underground reservoirs which can then be tapped by artesian bores. The Nullarbor Plain, a flat, barren, red and ochre vastness broken only by clumps of saltbush and wildflowers, has numerous, magnificent underground caves and sinkholes. Trees are few and far between, and the heat can be aggravated by powerful and fearsome dust storms. Sheep stations on the Nullarbor are large and isolated, and the few families who live on them have been braving the hardships for generations. When the rain fails to come, waterholes dry up and the ground becomes void of vegetation. Water has to be carried in huge tankers, and wool when clipped transported by truck or train on what is the world's longest straight stretch of rail, extending 500 kilometres without a bend.

Unlike the Nullarbor, the Barkly Tableland has forests of scraggy dust-covered trees, and treeless tracts where rich savanna grasses grow after the 'wet'. Cattle stations are huge — the world's largest being 'Alexandria' comprising over 21,000 square kilometres.

Another huge artesian basin, covering one and three quarter million square kilometres, extends west of the Eastern Highlands over an area incorporating parts of Queensland, Northern Territory and South Australia. It forms the Lake Eyre Basin, one of the world's largest inland drainage catchments, and is fed by the Cooper,

Diamantina, Mulligan and Georgina Rivers which disperse their evaporating loads into the numerous interconnecting channels that criss-cross the silted deltas of the Channel Country. The water that finally reaches the limestone of the Great Artesian Basin seeps to the underground shelf. After heavy rain or drainage, which generally occurs only one year in five, the red earth becomes a flourish of green grass and bright flowers which attract large numbers of birds and a deafening array of assorted insects.

On the fringes of the deserts and semi-arid regions, the hard sclerophyllous grasses merge into a scrub of mulga, acacias and hop bush. More birdlife and larger animals can be seen, and trees, gnarled as a result of the land's harshness, become less scarce.

To the north of the Channel Country, where the Gulf of Carpentaria meets Torres Strait, the terrain changes to a thick lush growth of grasses and mangrove swamps in the wet season. Among these and isolated trees are clusters of woodlands sprinkled between sand dunes and patches of tropical rainforests whose eucalyptus trees become amazingly semi-deciduous in the unquenchable 'dry'.

Here the hot wet summers on the predominantly flat plains make travel impossible. As the rivers swell and spill over their banks to form a shallow sea of water, debris and silt are carried and deposited in the reclaimed gulf swamps and muddy estuaries among which lurk the saltwater *Crocodilus porosus* and freshwater *Crocodilus johnstoni*. The 'wet' lasts about three months before the south-east trades bring back the hot 'dry'. The sun and evaporation then sap the moisture from the soggy plains as the deciduous trees shed their leaves and the grasslands become scorched and die. Most rivers, lagoons, billabongs and coastal channels dry up and all that can be seen of them are areas of baked cracked mud. Millions of birds head south and animals flock to the nearest permanent waterholes. The hardy eucalypts turn their scented leaves razor-edged to face the sun and most flowers disappear for another year.

Extending along the coast in a southerly direction, the neck of the Gulf Country merges to a backbone of rugged

Many houses in Queensland are raised from the ground on stilts to provide for extra coolness during the hot summer months. This Brisbane house offers a charming contrast to the high-rise buildings in the background.

Simply constructed bark huts provide shelter for the Aborigines of Arnhem Bay, Northern Territory.

A simple homestead near Geraldton, Western Australia.

uplifted ranges where steep jagged crags drop sheer to deep rift valleys. These Eastern Highlands run parallel to the coast as a relatively thin strip of plateau varying in height and width, separating the narrow belt of rich well-watered coastal plains on which half of Australia's population lives from the arid inland which is robbed of rainfall by their presence.

This long belt of highlands, moulded, carved and sculptured, is the result of faulting, folding, upthrust and some volcanic activity. Near Cairns in Queensland, the plateau with its numerous crater lakes rises to a high point of 1700 metres above sea level. Deep ravines and gorges have carved through the steep hard-rocked eastern scarps over which plunge numerous waterfalls. Vegetation, lush and often impenetrable, grows on rich soils fed by a humid climate. Most of the rivers drain on the eastern side of the range and flow short distances through deep fertile valleys to the sea. To the west of the divide, the extensive tableland slopes gently in rolling grass plains over which meander low gradient rivers, marked by rows of coolibahs, river red gums and acacias. The Norman and Flinders Rivers flow in a north and north-west direction and empty in the Gulf of Carpentaria; rivers such as the Georgina, Barcoo, Diamantina and Thomson run to the Channel Country from where they drain into the Great Artesian Basin; others such as Warrego, Nive, Langlo, Ward and Maranoa feed the great Murray River which leaves the continent at Murray Mouth, pushing into the Southern Ocean with great pressure waves of fresh water from its estuary, Lake Alexandrina — a massive buffer between ocean and river.

In Central Queensland the highlands level out to about 700 metres above sea level and bulge westward. These lower plateaux fail to trap the south-east trade winds and hence the much drier climate reduces the vegetation to extensive grasslands and savanna woodlands which feed a

massive cattle industry. Irrigated from artesian bores, sugar cane is grown extensively on the flat, richly silted plains. During excessive rains, the Haughton and Burdekin Rivers often burst their banks to flood thousands of square kilometres of 'patchwork' fields. In recent years, rice paddies have proved successful.

Further south, the Great Diving Range curves and

Lancelin, Western Australia. Commonly called grass-trees, yaccas and blackboys, these slow-growing trees with their charred leaf-base and grass-like leaves have been likened to Aborigines with spears.

These huge steel balls with connecting chains were dragged by heavy equipment to clear the forest areas around Tully, Queensland.

At Bonnie Rock, in the ancient Yilgarn area of Western Australia, this enormous cave was created when a huge slab of rock collapsed following the Meckering earthquake which occurred in October 1968, and registered 6.9 on the Richter Scale.

connects with a series of rugged tablelands: the Carnarvon Range, a group of wild basalt-capped sandstone ranges whose vertical cliffs rise in broken caverns and scarps to over 1000 metres; the Bunya Mountains, where bunya pines tower over the lush rainforest of the basalt upthrust; and the basalt-capped volcanic plateaux of the McPherson Range whose ruggedness has protected what is now the largest area of surviving temperate rainforest.

A raw turtle egg provides gourmet fare for this member of the Lardil tribe at Mornington Island in the Gulf of Carpentaria, who, prepared for a corroboree, wears the feathers of a white cockatoo as part of his head dress.

The jabiru is Australia's only stork and lives along the north and north-east coasts of the continent. Both male and female build the nest, incubate the eggs and feed their young, which they protect from intruders by shaking their bills to produce a loud clacking noise.

Carefree participants enjoy the boat races at Darwin's Beer Can Regatta.

To the west, the terrain slopes gently over 1500 kilometres to the Lake Eyre Basin; while the east is barred by steep forested escarpments which drop to fertile alluvial plains marked by rugged broken peaks or cores of volcanoes, tablelands, sand dunes and deep cutting rivers which become tidal about 60 kilometres before entering the ocean.

Along the coast, towns varying in population and size dot the landscape at close and regular intervals. To the west of the divide and on the range itself, the cattle population is large, but the towns are few and well separated.

In New South Wales, the Great Dividing Range becomes higher and more narrow. The New England Plateau with its isolated peaks of 1500 metres rises from a coast of river valleys that was once richly endowed in dense rainforest and magnificent stretches of golden beaches. Waterfalls cascade down the forest-covered escarpments. The western side is marked by a less steep escarpment which falls to flat plains which become drier the further west they extend.

To the south, the Central Tablelands border fertile river valleys separated by rugged ridges. Long sandy beaches curving to jutting headlands, extend for hundreds of kilometres, broken only by river mouths and natural harbours. The Blue Mountains, once a barrier for explorers, divides the coastal strip on which Sydney is situated from the vast rolling undulating sheep, cattle and wheat country which merges with the dry flat barren plains on their western side.

The Southern Highlands, still part of the chain of the Great Dividing Range, appear as the highest, most rugged wild mountain area in Australia. The tallest point on the plateau is Mount Kosciusko which rises to 2228 metres. In springtime, the melting of the extensive winter snowfields, far larger than those of Switzerland, feeds the turbulent Murray, Murrumbidgee and Snowy Rivers which carry water over much of south-east Australia. Dense eucalypt forests fringe the slopes to about 1800 metres. Above that only the hardy and beautiful snow gums appear as isolated monuments to nature. In spring, delicate alpine flowers carpet the slopes, while ferns, mosses, staghorns and other moisture-loving plants burrow into the steep gullies and waterpaths.

In Victoria, the deep granite belt with its steep gullies, glacial lakes and soaring peaks, narrows and reduces height on its western ridge. From this extends broad low-lying undulating river valleys bordering prosperous pastoral holdings and flourishing townships. South of these valleys the Victorian Hills, dominated by the wild and remote Grampians, swing in a west-east direction to eventually connect with the Victorian Alps.

South of the Alps, the highlands merge with the wild and beautiful country of Gippsland where dense forests

Stanwell Park, New South Wales. Much of Australia's south-east coast is characterised by a series of prominent hard-rock headlands indented with splended beaches which merge with the escarpments of the Great Dividing Range.

A rare white kangaroo and passenger make new friends.

Lord Howe Island is administratively part of New South Wales, but lies in the Pacific Ocean, approximately 700 kilometres north-east of Sydney. About 11 kilometres long and three kilometres at its broadest point, the island attracts an increasing number of tourists each year. It was discovered in February 1788 by Lieutenant Henry Lidgbird Ball, commander of the Supply who named it after the then British Colonial Secretary of State. Seen here is Mount Gower, which rises 866 metres above sea level.

meet a series of low-lying lakes, beaches, sand bars, submerged plains of mangrove, and marshes. Here along the coast, islands carved from the mainland provide sanctuaries for wildlife.

East of Melbourne, the Dandenong Ranges with their tall straight eucalypts, ferns and flowers, provide essential breathing space for the sprawling metropolis. Near here the Great Dividing Range dips and continues on the southern side of Bass Strait to terminate at Australia's most southerly point.

Moulded by geological upheavals and sculptured by glacial movement, the vast areas of Tasmania's highlands remain grand, forbidding and remote. Wild forest-covered mountainous ranges contrast with an equally high but flat treeless plateau dotted with hundreds of clear blue crater lakes. Most of Australia's alpine flora and fauna live on this awesome landscape which feeds the Derwent River

At Lockhart, New South Wales, this memorial, made of wool-bales and wagonwheels, is dedicated to the wool pioneers of the district.

The Balconies on Mount Victory in the Grampian Ranges, Victoria.

Situated in north-west Queensland, Mount Isa is a centre for the production of silver-lead, zinc and copper. The mining field was discovered by John Campbell Miles in 1923 after which hundreds of lessees operated small mines. Within two years the Mount Isa Mines Limited had taken over all leases. With its railway connection to the east, Mount Isa is also an important centre for the cattle industry.

Stark red and squeezed into a series of folds, the MacDonnell Ranges in the south-western corner of the Northern Territory rise sheer from the plains. The ranges extend about 380 kilometres, and are approximately 65 kilometres wide. Discovered by John McDouall Stuart in 1860, they were named after the South Australian Governor and are often referred to as the 'core of the centre'.

and its tributaries. Winters are cold with sleet and snow, but in spring the flowers enliven the rich, green Tamar Valley and the midlands. Caves and drowned river valleys lie in the deeply dissected south-eastern region.

With an area of 67,897 square kilometres, Tasmania is the country's largest island and only island State. Its very location and landforms ensures howling cold westerly winds which whip over its small area and lash the oceans

against its eroding sides. In the shallow waters of Bass Strait, two groups of islands are the remaining links in chains of mountains that once formed land bridges between Tasmania and Victoria.

The icy waters of the Southern Ocean hug the stark mainland cliffs which are broken by the shallow entrances of Western Port and Port Phillip Bay on which Melbourne stands. Westward from Cape Otway, the coastline becomes

Enterprise takes many forms. This sign was seen at Ettalong near Gosford, New South Wales.

Windsor, New South Wales, under flood, March 1978.

pocketed with sheltered sand beaches which contrast with the impressive limestone stacks at Port Campbell. Islands mark the shores which turn to swamps further west. Inland, volcanic plains, over which Mount Gambier and its crater Blue Lake preside, run to the mudflats which continue west, forming a series of lakes and peninsulas as far as the wonderful wildlife region of The Coorong. This narrow strip of water which runs parallel with the coast for 140 kilometres, is separated from the ocean by a thin sand stretch known as Younghusband Peninsula. Sand dunes appear to the north, and to the west sits the Huge Lake Alexandrina into which the Murray River empties.

A series of peninsulas, gulfs and islands break the sweep of coastline near Adelaide. The shallow gulfs and narrow coastal plains are bounded by long rugged peninsulas predominated by salt lakes or rugged precipices. Fertile valleys tucked among the ranges produce cattle, wine, fruit and sheep. To the north, the Flinders Ranges meets the desert, while to the west stretches the vast, arid Nullarbor Plain. At the western extremity of the Great Australian Bight, a mass of low-lying islands called Recherche Archipelago dot the waters for hundreds of kilometres.

Around Western Australia's south-west fringe, huge forests of eucalypts, kauri and jarrah extend to the fertile region on which Perth stands. A narrow coastal plain of limestone and sandstone, it is fed by waters from the Darling Range whose scarp runs parallel with the coast.

Timber, dairying, sheep and orchards are important industries on what is Western Australia's richest agricultural land.

On the dangerous Kimberley coast, gorges, bays, estuaries and harbours line the knotted, broken foreshores. Islands and coral reefs are numerous in the warm waters and the difference of about 10 metres in daily tidal levels results in vast mud flats and stranded marine life at low tide. Cyclonic summer rains are common and during the 'wet', the long rivers burst their banks and cover several kilometres but are reduced to a series of mud-cracked puddles in the 'dry' when temperatures and evaporation rates are high.

From the coastal plains the Napier Ranges rise in the north as sheer walls into which magnificent gorges have been cut by fast-flowing rivers. Grass covered, and wooded in parts, they run for hundreds of kilometres in a northwest-southeast direction. Behind them, the King Leopold Ranges, the highest plateaux in Western Australia, eventually meet the dissected plains, plateaux, gorges and swamps of the north and west. Huge tracts of grassland provide fuel for fires in the hot dry season. To the north of the State, the Kimberleys are noted for the vast cattle stations from where beef is transported to Darwin and overseas. Pioneers of the area fought the harsh climate, hostile Aborigines and isolation. Families such as the Duracks pushed stock overland from Queensland across drought-ridden deserts to take up land in the lush Kimberleys.

At a rodeo at Terrey Hills, Sydney, people and steers scramble in all directions, the objective being the capture of a ribbon attached to the horns of one of the beasts.

Theseus conquering the Minotaur, a detail of the Archibald Fountain in Sydney's Hyde Park. To commemorate the alliance between Australia and France during World War I, Jules Francois Archibald, founder of the weekly magazine, The Bulletin, *bequeathed money for a memorial of bronze to be sculptured. The work was commenced in 1926, and presented to the people of Sydney in March 1933, having cost $12,864 to complete.*

Darwin and the islands to the north are provided with fine climate and a wealth of wildlife. Here, the coast has many indentations and sandy beaches but few large estuaries. The low desert dunes and mud flats of the Gulf of Carpentaria are fringed with islands and coral cays, while in the Torres Strait, islands that had once formed part of the Great Dividing Range, dot the perimeter of Cape York Peninsula.

One of Australia's most spectacular attractions is the Great Barrier Reef. This beautiful maze of colour, texture and wildlife forms an intricately balanced ecosystem which has survived and grown for thousands of years. It is the largest of the world's coral reefs, extending southward from Torres Strait parallel with the coast for a distance of approximately 2000 kilometres.

Each of these thousands of individual reefs is made up of limestone which is produced as a means of protection by millions of minute animals called polyps. These builders form a layer over the non-living coral and require temperatures of between 20° - 30°, light, oxygen and plankton on which to feed. None can survive long periods uncovered by water, excessive freshwater inflow or sediment disturbances. There are hundreds of species of coral, each having a different shape, texture and colour.

Sailing on Crawley Bay, near Perth, Western Australia. The University of Western Australia can be seen in the background.

The long-snouted bilby, or rabbit bandicoot, is a nocturnal marsupial which burrows deep into the soil and lives largely on insects and small animals. Once plentiful in New South Wales, South Australia and Western Australia, their numbers have been depleted substantially by the depredations of the fox and men who once hunted them for their pelts.

The drifting coastal dunes at Eucla, Western Australia, have almost swallowed the sandstone buildings of the repeating telegraph station which began operating in 1877 as part of the Adelaide-Albany Overland Telegraph Line. About 20 kilometres from the South Australian border, the site was chosen because of a permanent well and/or fine extensive harbour, both of which are rare commodities along the Great Australian Bight.

The Great Barrier Reef supports an abundance of wildlife. An infinite variety of fish and other marine creatures varying in size, shape, features and habits, live among the coral and plant life. Skeletons of ships wrecked on the reefs testify to the hazards of the waters.

As well as the coral reefs and cays of the region, high or continental islands emerge as rugged land masses composed generally of the same material as the nearby mainland and with similar vegetation. Fringed by reefs, they are often mountain tops which have become separated by the rise of water. Such is the case with Norfolk and Lord Howe Islands. Situated off the coast of New South Wales, both are the remains of a chain of volcanic mountains long since separated from the coast. Lord Howe Island is about 12 kilometres in length. Like Norfolk Island, 1000 kilometres to its north-east, its cliffs are steep, and about one-third of its plant life is indigenous to the island.

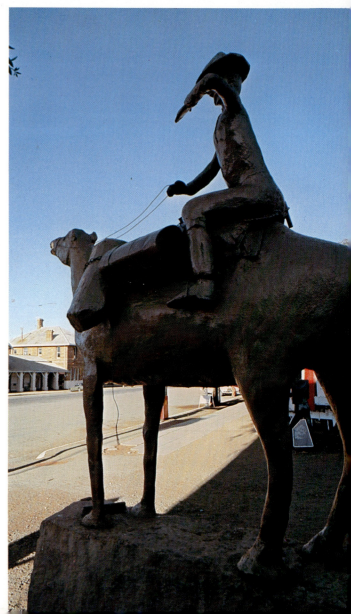

A family of emus near Hamilton, Victoria. A flightless bird with small wings, the emu uses his legs as defence, is capable of running long distances quickly and is a strong swimmer.

A monument to the pioneers and forming part of an open-air museum at Coolgardie, Western Australia. When large deposits of gold were discovered in the vicinity in 1892, 15,000 people were attracted to the desolate area. During the boom years, the town boasted of three breweries, twenty-six hotels, two stock exchanges and many impressive Government buildings. Water, ever-scarce was transported by camel trains and sold for one shilling a gallon.

The bets are taken at the Merriwa, New South Wales, picnic races.

At Cocklebiddy, halfway between Eucla and Norseman, Western Australia, on the Nullarbor Plain's Eyre Highway, a lone cyclist continues his long overland haul from Perth to Sydney.

A huge river gum near Wagga Wagga, New South Wales, continues to live even though its core has been destroyed. It has the largest base of any known tree in the Riverina.

The waratah is the floral emblem of New South Wales, and is most commonly found around Sydney, Newcastle and the south coast of New South Wales.

The brilliantly coloured crimson rosella feeds on berries and the seeds of wattles and eucalypts along much of Australia's east and south-east coasts.

Australia has thousands of unique plants and animals. There are about 500 species of eucalypt, and more than 600 types of wattle. Pines, figs, bottle or baobab trees, palms, cycads, grass-trees or blackboys, banksias, angopheras; and plants like mulga scrub, salt bush, wiry spinifex, creepers, ivies and mosses — each imparting character to the region in which it grows, whether it be desert or rainforest, mountains or the coastal plains.

Australia has no indigenous hoofed animals, but the large numbers of marsupials, monotremes and mammals symbolise to many people the identity of this continent. Birds, too, are profuse in variety, colour, size and splendour. Some of these creatures are becoming smaller in numbers as their habitats are destroyed or predators increase. This also applies to reptiles, insects and spiders — all of whom form part of a complicated ecosystem. Our fish, seals, whales, dugongs, sponges, jellyfish and scavengers are subjected to increased pollution of their waters.

The Aborigines knew the art of survival and lived in harmony with nature. As nomads their lifestyle left little area for possessions. From generation to generation they passed down their music, dances and legends. They gathered fruit and roots, and hunted birds, land animals

The strange festered surface of the opal fields of Andamooka, South Australia. To escape the searing heat, many prospectors live underground in disused mines.

Gemstones taken from the ground at Andamooka, South Australia. When extracted from the soil, the opal is an anomalous piece of silica containing water. With special tools and skill, it is then cut and polished to become a beautiful and valuable gem.

From a rough piece of stone found in the Andamooka opal fields, love and skill have worked a miraculous transformation.

In a treeless, arid landscape where heat and flies are almost beyond endurance, the 'galvo' homes of some of Andamooka's opal miners impart a uniquely Australian character.

Coober Pedy in South Australia is an opal mining centre. Houses such as this, carved out of the hillside, and those converted from disused mines, gave rise to the Aboriginal name, Coober Pedy, which means 'white man's hole in the ground'. Opals have been mined in the area for more than 60 years.

and sea creatures only to eat and keep warm. They grew nothing and never disturbed the soil. Never would they decimate an area of each species of food — the land looked after them, and they in no way raped the land. For thousands, perhaps millions of years they were part of the intricate influences and inter-relationships between landforms, climate, soil, vegetation and animals that moulded the country. Then came the European man and with him the need for change.

Free advice on a Sydney suburban thoroughfare.

At Kempton, Tasmania, a pair of Bennett's Wallabies show curiosity and timidity. In the early years of settlement they were slaughtered extensively for sport and meat.

The dingo, also known as warrigal, is a wild dog thought to have been introduced to Australia thousands of years ago by the Aborigines. Regarded as a pest, it has been ruthlessly hunted for bounties, but plentiful numbers still live in isolated areas.

To many scholars, and superstitious sailors, Australia was a myth, *Terra Australis Incognita*, the unknown land to the south whose secrets were guarded by the dangerous uncharted oceans. For those who understood the dangerous currents and prevailing winds, trade was welcome. Indonesian trepang fishermen and Melanesian voyagers are known to have sailed their small crafts to and from Australia's north coast. However, until the beginning of the 16th Century, Europe knew very little of the lands south of the equator. With the constant search for new markets, European exploration became very active at about this time. In 1606, the crew of the Dutch ship *Duyfken*, captained by Willem Jansz, made what was probably the first European landfall on the Australian mainland. Jansz, who had been following New Guinea's south coast, missed the Torres Strait and landed at Cape Keerweer (Cape Turn Again) in the Gulf of Carpentaria. Believing he was still in New Guinea, Jansz was not impressed with the desolate land and described the inhabitants as 'wild, cruel black savages'. A few months

later, the Portuguese explorer, Luis Vaez de Torres, sailing the *Almiranta*, discovered the dangerous Torres Strait.

It was the west coast that was next to be discovered, again by accident. A new, faster and safer sea route from

Magnificent stands of eucalypts near Olinda, Victoria. East of Melbourne, the rich volcanic soil of the Dandenong Range, in conjunction with heavy rainfall, has created a beautiful bush native garden which is the home of much wildlife.

Bounded to the east, north and west by saltpans, sand dunes and gibbers, the Flinders Ranges in South Australia extend from just south of Lake Eyre to Port Pirie, a distance of approximately 400 kilometres. The heavily dissected protrusion was discovered by Matthew Flinders in March 1802, and later explored by Edward Eyre.

Palm Beach, north of Sydney, with the Pacific Ocean and the still waters of Pittwater separated by an isthmus of sand culminating in a rocky outcrop on which stands Barrenjoey Lighthouse.

The Wrest Point Hotel, housing the first legal casino in Australia, is a dominant feature of suburban Hobart.

Africa to the East was found in 1611 by Henrik Brouwer, who, to avoid the doldrums, struck east from Cape of Good Hope and encountered strong westerly winds. A few thousand kilometres further, he turned north for Java. His discovery became a popular route and five years later Dirk Hartog, travelling the same course, miscalculated his westerly run and landed about 725 kilometres north of Perth on an island to which he gave his name.

More ships came. Those which were not wrecked turned north and sailed parallel with the treacherous coast. Officers named landmarks, made maps and gave unkind reports of the country they sighted.

In 1623 the Dutch Governor of Amboina sent the ships *Arnhem* and *Pera* to follow and extend the course the *Duyfken* had taken 17 years before. The *Arnhem* landed at what is now Arnhem Land, where her crew had a skirmish with natives.

Most of the early explorers found the coastline, with its underwater reefs and hidden rocks, violent storms, strong currents, heavy surfs and gales, highly dangerous. It became a graveyard for many ships and sailors. The land was consistently described as dry and barren; the people fearsome.

It was Abel Tasman who discovered Tasmania in 1642. Having sighted its western shore and named the island after Anthony van Diemen, Governor-General of the Dutch East Indies, he sailed around the southern point to the eastern coast.

Others followed. William de Vlamingh named the Swan River in Western Australia and William Dampier's reports aroused interest in Great Britain.

In 1770, James Cook sailed south from Tahiti to New Zealand in his ship *Endeavour*. He charted the coastline and made contact with the natives then sailed west, hoping to link with Tasman's course along the east coast of Van Diemen's Land. His plans were foiled by winds and currents but at six o'clock in the morning of 20th April, 1770, Lieutenant Zachary Hicks sighted land near Cape Everard. They turned north, charting and naming landmarks along the coast.

When Cook's party landed at Botany Bay, a few natives fled. Two others threw spears at the trespassers before being driven off by gunfire. Botanist Joseph Banks and others busied themselves collecting specimens, drawing and noting trees, flowers and wildlife. After some further exploration to the north, Cook sailed for home, but not before raising the flag and claiming the east coast for England.

Although much interest was aroused by Cook's findings, there was, however, no urgency to colonise Australia until after Britain lost the War of Independence and hence her American Territories.

Discovered in 1876 by John Doyle, the Barron Falls on the Atherton Tableland's eastern escarpment, lies about 17 kilometres from the mouth of the Barron River, north of Cairns, Queensland.
Spectacular in flood, its flow is normally controlled by the release of water from the Tinaroo Dam. Its reliability and velocity resulted in Australia's first underground hydro station being built in 1935.

Recently under threat of demolition, the magnificent Palace Hotel in Perth, Western Australia, depicts the affluence, charm and beauty of a by-gone era.

The Merriwa country races, New South Wales. In isolated areas the picnic races are an eagerly awaited social event.

The unusual interior of the Cathedral of St Francis Xavier at Geraldton, Western Australia. Designed by Father John Hawes in 1913, the church has been described as 'a poem in stone'.

The Dora Dora Hotel at Talmalmo, New South Wales.

Rigging for the race on Batemans Bay, New South Wales. Sailing is one of the most popular sports in Australia.

Near the Murrumbidgee River at Gundagai, New South Wales, a drover and his dogs move a flock of sheep. In the early days of Australia vast empires were built around the fine, newly discovered lands and much of the nation's wealth was carried on the sheeps' back.

Needing to relieve the overcrowded prisons, Britain decided to despatch convicted men and women to Botany Bay where a penal settlement under military control would be formed. Under the command of Arthur Phillip, 11 convict ships set sail for the great unknown land to the south.

Botany Bay was reached on 18th January, 1788. The area however, proved unsuitable and the settlement was transferred to Sydney Cove. Tents were soon erected and a building programme begun. Simple shelters were constructed of wattle-and-daub, bark and thatching, and it it soon became apparent that the number of skilled craftsmen and tradesmen were few. Tools also were inadequate and the lack of initiative by the majority of these 'First Fleeters' hampered progress. The military organised the work and the convicts reluctantly carried out the tasks. The climate was harsh, and mosquitoes, flies and ants combined with intense heat proved unbearable. Crops failed. Government cattle were lost and the majority of breeding stock died. Floods had preceded droughts and people were hungry, poorly clothed, diseased and of low morale.

As an incentive to ex-soldiers and convicts who had completed their sentences, Governor Phillip offered land grants in newly found good farming areas, but few knew much about farming. The officers were unco-operative, and with more and more convicts arriving, the Governor found it difficult to administer the Colony.

When Phillip left, the settlement fell into the clutches of the New South Wales Corps which monopolised trade and prospered at the expense of the people. Land was granted to officers, with convicts assigned to work for them at the expense of the commissariat. Rum became the accepted means of payment and illicit stills were rife. The Colony stagnated and became more corrupt while the officers grew more wealthy.

Those governors who followed and tried to smash the economic and civil control of the military officers, and resume order, justice and law, were opposed, challenged and their orders not enforced. It wasn't until Governor Macquarie arrived with his 73rd Highlanders Regiment to replace the Corps, that major changes were enforced.

With extensive oil drilling on the north-west shelf of Australia, Fremantle provides an excellent port for ocean-going oil rigs. It is Western Australia's only major port and has enormous specially-designed berthing facilities to handle the increasing traffic.

With so many fine surfing beaches and generally favourable climatic conditions, body surfing and boardriding have become popular sports among all age groups in Australia.

A strange, nimble and beautifully marked marsupial, the numbat, or banded ant-eater, feeds on termites which it extracts from trees by a succession of rapid flicks of the tongue. It is now found only in the south of Western Australia and the north-west part of South Australia.

Fringed by dramatic limestone cliffs, beside which lies the graveyard of many ships, the flat-topped Nullarbor plateau was first crossed in 1841 by Edward John Eyre. Extending parallel with the Great Australian Bight for about 550 kilometres and inland to a depth of approximately 250 kilometres, this treeless area abounds in wildflowers, saltbush and bluebush. The porous nature of the surface limestone soaks up the small amount of rain, and while there are no surface streams, there are a number of underground lakes and sinkholes.

In the Northern Territory, where cattle stations cover vast areas and fencing is economically unfeasible, tick-resistant Brahmin cattle are mustered by helicopter to a point where horsemen take over. The prosperity of many of the large properties in the Territory fluctuate according to the climate and market conditions. It is an industry where people can either make or lose fortunes.

Australia has many distinctive and beautiful flowers, one being the acorn banksia, which grows in sandy soil around Perth, Western Australia. There are over 50 species of banksia in Australia, each differing in size, colour, shape and composition.

Meanwhile, other discoveries and settlements had been made. Norfolk Island had been self-supporting since shortly after Governor Phillip had despatched Lieutenant King to secure it for the Colony. George Bass had sailed through Bass Strait and with Matthew Flinders, in 1798, had circumnavigated Van Diemen's Land. Three years later in the *Investigator* Flinders began his journey of charting and circumnavigating Australia, an accomplishment that was later followed by Phillip Parker King.

Fear of French intentions had been aroused when the ships *Le Geographe* and *Le Naturaliste* began exploring the coasts of Western Australia, South Australia and Tasmania. Governor King hastily sent Lieutenant John Bowen to Van Diemen's Land to form a settlement on the Derwent River. In 1804, Lieutenant-Colonel David Collins with a party of convicts, marines and free settlers, landed at the site of what was to become Hobart. In November of that year, Lieutenant-Colonel Paterson was sent to form a settlement in the north to watch Bass Strait and safeguard the sealing industry. The site eventually chosen became Launceston.

Cotton harvesting at Wee Waa on the north-west plains of New South Wales. Cotton seed was first introduced in Australia by settlers from the First Fleet who had little success in growing the plant in Sydney.

This tiger snake, caught on Cat Island in Bass Strait, will be sent to the Reptile Park at Gosford, New South Wales. There are more than 100 species of snakes in Australia, some of them venomous. The tiger snake is one of Australia's most deadly reptiles.

In the Darwin Beer Can Regatta, craft constructed of sealed beer cans compete for the honours. These boats are propelled by various means, from oars to powerful motors.

The Olgas are a series of conglomerate domes, the highest rising about 450 metres above the surrounding plain. Situated south of Lake Amadeus and about 320 kilometres south-west of Alice Springs, the 30 domes, separated by narrow vertical chasms, were first sighted in October 1872 by Ernest Giles who described them as 'monstrous pink haystacks, leaning for support against one another'.

About 40 kilometres east of the Olgas lies Ayers Rock, the dome of a buried hill which has been smoothed by winds. Rising 335 metres above the sandy plains, and about 8 kilometres in circumference at the base, it is the world's largest single rock. It is a popular tourist attraction, and an important feature in the mythology of the local Aborigines, the cave paintings with which the monolith is decorated bearing testimony to this. Ayers Rock was sighted in 1872 by Ernest Giles and named a year later by William Gosse. The Aborigines called it Uluru.

Mount Connor, Northern Territory, is one of three giant tors lying in a straight line. Situated on a flat sandy plain about 120 kilometres east of the Olgas, it is a flat-topped oval-shaped mesa, about 3½ kilometres long by about 1 kilometre wide, and rises in sheer vertical cliffs to about 300 metres. The remains of a pioneer's house sits in a field of spinifex grass.

Flowing only after heavy rains, the Todd River at Alice Springs, Northern Territory, is the venue for the Centre's annual Bang Tay Muster. In 1872, Alice Springs, then called Stuart, operated as a repeater station on the Darwin-Adelaide Overland Telegraph Line.

Set against a background of red earth, red mountains and the brilliant blue Northern Territory sky, the stark white ghost gums stand out in clear relief.

Living in forest areas of north-east Queensland and New Guinea, the tree kangaroo has shortish hindfeet and large well-developed forearms which it uses for climbing and leaping among branches.

On Elcho Island, separated from Arnhem Land, Northern Territory, by the Cadell Strait, Aboriginal artist, Wadamou, paints a legend in bark.

Windsurfing on Australia's waterways has become a popular sport. At Belmont, near Newcastle, New South Wales, the races attract large crowds of spectators.

The Australian fur seal is found on the south-east mainland and Tasmanian coast. Its pelt and oil became sought after from 1798 when the sealing industry in Australia began. They are now protected.

Under a record-breaking blanket of snow, Queanbeyan, New South Wales, was first settled in 1828 but gained importance when Canberra was established a short distance away. It is a wool-growing and mixed farming area through which flows the Queanbeyan River.

A carpet of yellow flowers covers the red sandy desert at Everard Station, South Australia. After rain the country blooms.

With his horse under the shade of a coolibah tree, an Aboriginal stockman at Waterloo Station, Northern Territory, watches a herd of grazing cattle.

The Durack Range in the north-west of Western Australia. Spectacular stony tablelands thrust up from a flat extensive valley. Producing cattle to supply the Wyndham abattoirs, much of the area has been subjected to experimental cropping following the damming of the Ord River.

Brisbane skyline – tall buildings reach for the sky on the banks of the Brisbane River.

Australia is one of the largest wheat producing countries in the world. This crop is growing in western New South Wales.

A grave in the cemetery at Mount Morgan, Queensland.

Cassilis, New South Wales. Foxes are not native to Australia, but were imported during the 1840's by the more well-heeled settlers for hunting purposes. Since then they have spread throughout the country, and because of their predatory habits, have become regarded as a pest with, in most places, a bounty on their skins.

Cattle crossing the Davidson River at Tully, north Queensland. Tully lies in a tropical rainforest strip of coastal plain which has been known to receive over 7000 mm of water within a year.

The beach at Manly, New South Wales. Manly was named by Governor Phillip who was impressed by the manly bearing of the area's Aborigines. The Norfolk Island pines which line the beach were planted between 1882 and 1884.

The black swan, the emblem of Western Australia, was first sighted in 1697 by the Dutch explorer Willem de Vlamingh. The Swan River at Perth is named because of them.

The two communities strived for self support. At first the land proved kind then poor conditions combined with a famine experienced in New South Wales, left Tasmania with little food and fewer hopes. Hunting parties were formed and the Government bought kangaroo meat from whoever could get it. The situation was intensified in 1805 when the people of Norfolk Island were resettled in Van Diemen's Land. Bushrangers became a threat and Aborigines showed discontent at the mass slaughter of their own food supply. Relief eventually arrived and the business of the island resumed. The whaling and sealing industry boomed, wool proved profitable, ship-making became lucrative and the community enjoyed a reasonably prosperous time.

In Sydney, Macquarie began cleaning up. Streets were widened, and public buildings erected at a rapid rate. Graft and corruption were minimised as new methods of Government trading were introduced. Emancipists and free settlers were encouraged to farm. Plans for townships were laid out, surveyed, then building begun. Roads into country areas were repaired and new ones made. Social activities were encouraged. Macquarie imported a monetary system to reduce bartering and replace rum as currency. To aid this and to stop the use of promissory notes, store receipts and other currencies, he organised a group of settlers to subscribe to and operate a bank, which became known as the Bank of New South Wales. Industries grew and new ones were formulated. Whaling and sealing brought vast wealth, and the wool industry rapidly expanded.

In the Victorian Dandenongs, the artist, William Ricketts, established a sanctuary in the peace of the surrounding rainforest. These sensitively sculptured figures emerge from the earth to harmonise so well with the natural environment.

The flower of Western Australia's Eucalyptus macrocarpa myrtaceae.

Queenstown on Tasmania's west coast is a copper mining town. Pyritic smelting has caused a constant sulphur haze to hang over the valley.

Calf-roping at a country rodeo. The horse pulls on the rope while the stockman drops the calf to mark it.

Limestone formations in the Pinnacles Desert, Western Australia. The strange shapes were caused by rain re-depositing lime from leached sand dunes to the roots of plants which have then become fossilised. Over the years this has accumulated, and with the disappearance of the loose surrounding sand, the desert graveyard has been exposed.

A hunter returns to camp with the day's catch. Derby, Western Australia.

Kangaroos silhouetted against the setting sun, Mudgee, New South Wales.

The kookaburra, laughing jackass, is a bird of formidable distinction.

Boxing kangaroos. Many years have passed since these all-Australian hopes William Dampier likened to a 'sort of racoon' and James Cook described as 'an animal something less than a greyhound, of a mouse colour, very slender made and swift of foot', last appeared in the prize-fighting ring.

Carn Brae, an old home in Port Pirie, South Australia.

Constructed of hand-made bricks, timber and thatched straw, this cottage standing in the working museum of Old Sydney Town, near Gosford, New South Wales, is a replica of those built in Sydney Cove in the early 1800's.

Tucked among the ferns and eucalypts is this attractive weatherboard house at Olinda, Victoria.

An oasis on the Birdsville Track. It was waterholes, and later artesian bores, which enabled cattle to be driven from south west Queensland to the Adelaide market.

At the foot of Mount Gillen, a few kilometres north of Tennant Creek in the Northern Territory, a giant granite monolith called Devil's Marble marks the grave of the Rev. John Flynn, who founded the Flying Doctor Service in 1928.

The craggy razor-edged Breadknife looms majestically over the Warrumbungle National Park, New South Wales. Sighted in 1818 by John Oxley, the incredible towering peaks are volcanic cones which have eroded over millions of years to their present form.

An old hop house on the Derwent River at New Norfolk, Tasmania. Hops were first introduced to Australia in 1803 and planted in Tasmania two years later. Today, the Derwent Valley with its alluvial soil and suitable climate produces most of Australia's hops.

The statue of Colonel William Light, which was erected in 1905, overlooks Adelaide, the city he founded and surveyed.

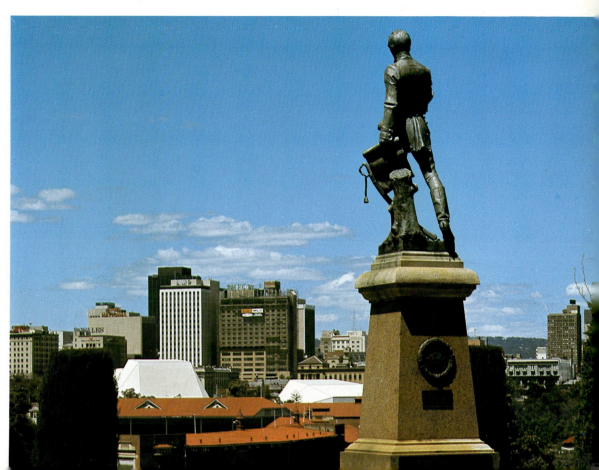

The Pieman River at Corinna on the wild west coast of Tasmania. It received its name from an escaped convict, Jimmy the Pieman, who was recaptured near the river.

Girls from the Bondi, Sydney, branch of the Royal Lifesaving Association practise their rescue procedures in preparation for future surf carnivals.

Peaceful coexistence at Swan Hill, Victoria.

A wallaby near Swan Hill, Victoria, basks peacefully in the sun.

On the border of Northern Territory and South Australia near the Musgrave Ranges, wildflowers flourish in the desert soil after spring rain.

An old steam train pulls out from the station at Timbertown, a village reconstructed to show how the early timber-getters lived and worked. Wauchope, New South Wales.

'Five minutes to start' on Botany Bay. This famous bay is crowded with boats all weekend.

Pyalong, Victoria. The debris at the foot of the railway bridge is indicative of flash flooding which occurs in many of Australia's rivers and creeks.

The sandstone Hampden Bridge in the Kangaroo Valley, New South Wales, is an outstanding early example of suspension bridgework in Australia.

A detail of the stone bridge crossing the Macquarie River at Ross, Tasmania.

Ross Bridge in Tasmania was built between 1833 and 1836 by convict labour.

The Cataract Gorge, Launceston, Tasmania.

The limestone caves at Hastings, Tasmania.

The Brisbane agricultural and horticultural annual show attracts a large crowd of spectators and exhibitors.

There had been many attempts to cross the Blue Mountains, but it wasn't until 1813 when Gregory Blaxland, William Lawson and William Charles Wentworth, taking with them four men, four horses and five dogs, achieved this by following the ridges rather than the valleys to cross the Great Dividing Range. Their success was soon marked by a road over which graziers took their stock west to new pasturing grounds.

Macquarie examined the rich pastures and sited the town of Bathurst. He sent Surveyor George Evans to follow the Macquarie River which resulted in the discovery of the Lachlan River and more land being taken for sheep. The New South Wales coast was explored and penal settlements formed at Newcastle and Port Macquarie. In the wake of all the discoveries moved the pioneers — usually the sheep men.

Macquarie left Australia in 1822. He had once said, 'I found New South Wales a jail and left it a Colony. I found a population of idle prisoners, paupers and paid officials, and left a large free community thriving in the produce of flocks and the labour of convicts.'

England had once again become worried by the possibilities of the French establishing a settlement in Australia. In 1817 Lieutenant Phillip Parker King was ordered to survey the continent's north coast and advise on possible areas for settlement. The site of Port Essington was chosen and a convict and military post, headed by Captain James Bremer, who formally took possession of the north between 130° and 135°, was established in 1824. This was later transferred to Melville Island.

Further French activity provoked London to instruct Governor Darling to form settlements on the coast north of Sydney, the New Holland coast and Western Port. Towards the end of 1823, John Oxley chose the site of Moreton Bay which he called Brisbane. A year later a penal settlement was formed and convicts from Newcastle and Port Macquarie were transported there. Norfolk Island was hastily reoccupied. No free settlers were allowed. It was to be a penal settlement for the worst of

Found in fresh water along Australia's eastern coastal belt, the amphibious duck-billed platypus is a uniquely Australian mammal. Its powerful front feet with which it swims also enable it to dig out the long burrow in which it lives, and its hind legs act as a form of stabiliser. The male platypus has a poisonous spur on the inside of the claw. The female lays eggs and the young, when hatched, suck milk from mammary gland ducts.

On Mount House cattle station in the Kimberley Ranges of Western Australia, an Aboriginal drover stops beside a baobab tree. Described by Ernestine Hill in her book, The Great Australian Loneliness *as 'a Caliban of a tree, a grizzled, distorted old goblin — a friendly ogre of the great North-west', this huge baobab which grows in sandy plains, yields a fruit which offers a reservoir of sustenance for the inland traveller.*

the convicts. Western Port proved inadequate and the settlement was abandoned in 1827, one year after its birth.

In 1826 Major Edmund Lockyer was sent to form a post at Albany, Western Australia. The following year Captain James Stirling examined the Swan River area with the prospect of forming a settlement there. His report to England was enthusiastic, and it wasn't long before Captain Fremantle was ordered to sail 'to the Swan River on the Western Coast of New South Wales, where you will on your arrival take formal possession of that part of the coast in the name of His Majesty, which possession is meant to be extended to the whole of the Western Coast.'

Britain agreed to a business proposition whereby one million acres at 1/6 an acre would be made available to a syndicate who guaranteed to meet all developing and settlement costs. Immigrants were to be granted 40 acres of land for every £3's worth of of securities or possessions landed. There were to be no convicts and all costs would be met by the immigrant. Stirling was appointed Governor.

However, the beginnings weren't easy. Settlers, ill-prepared for the mammoth task of clearing and farming virgin land arrived faster than the land could be surveyed. Labour was short, Aborigines became hostile and much of the land was infertile. There were no facilities or roads, as no tradesmen had been imported. A large number of investors had never farmed before, and many quit and returned to England. Much money was invested but few made their money pay. Although vast areas had been alloted, there was very little cultivation. The settlement battled on with sickness, poor diet, lack of progress and depressed capital providing little incentive.

In 1849, needing British support and finance, Western Australia became a Crown Colony. As the transportation of convicts from England to New South Wales had ended in 1840, new areas to send them were needed, and Western Australia welcomed them as much-needed labour. Together with an inflow of free tradesmen, the transportations continued until 1868.

South Australia was founded in 1834 by an Act of Parliament. In proposing a scheme for the new settlement, Edward Gibbon Wakefield reasoned that if land was fixed at such a price that only the minority of people could afford to purchase, plenty of labour would thus be ensured. There would be no convicts and no land grants. His plan drew much attention in England. It was proposed that the money spent purchasing the land would be used to import immigrants who would work on the farms. The Government agreed to try the scheme on condition that land to the value of £35,000 be presold and £20,000 invested with the Government as security. As land in the other colonies was much cheaper, inducements to invest in the new Colony were difficult to make. John Hindmarsh was appointed Governor and Colonel William Light Surveyor-General. Light chose the site for Adelaide

Elcho Island, Northern Territory. In recent times there has been a marked population increase in many Aboriginal tribes due to the change of tribal customs.

Cairns, with its splendid harbour, Trinity Bay, was settled in 1876 and named after William Cairns, Governor of Queensland. During World War II, Trinity Inlet became an important Catalina flying boat base.

Prominent naturalist Vincent Serventy and Keith Fletcher examine one of the few remaining Aboriginal tree carvings near Manildra, New South Wales. Many of these trees, usually found in threes to indicate a burial ground, have been cut down and the carvings transferred to a museum for safety.

A prospector's bush shower in the hot desert region of King's Canyon, Northern Territory.

and work began. People, flocking to the area before surveys could be done, could not understand why, as free British settlers, they were not entitled to self-government. Management was difficult as control was delegated between the Colonial Office and a board of Commissioners, most of whom resided in England and had little knowledge of problems and situations in Australia. Only a small amount of land was productive, and within four years a depression faced the country. South Australia became bankrupt.

The British Government took over, paid all the debts, cut expenditure and wages. Taxes and working hours were increased, and with no relief funds for those unemployed, people hastily sought work on farms. By 1846, the wool, grain and some copper mining industries were prospering, and in 1856, South Australia achieved self-government.

The Fitzroy River flows through the Geikie Gorge in the southern part of the Kimberley Ranges, Western Australia.

The Town Hall, Perth, Western Australia.

Clothes props and dunnies on the vast desolate Nullarbor Plain.

Wheat farmers at Grenfell, New South Wales, await their turn at the silos to discharge their loads of grain.

On the road to Thredbo, one of New South Wales' Snowy Mountain ski resorts.

An enormous area of Western Australia and the Northern Territory consists of monotonous red gibber plains and infinite sand dunes which produce little all-year-round vegetation other than porcupine spinifex grass. However, it is hoped as a result of extensive exploration, the area may soon be producing significant quantities of oil.

Hamilton, Victoria. Cricket is a game not to be laughed at in Australia.

Found along the eastern coast from the islands of Bass Strait to south-east Queensland, the common wombat is a large marsupial which digs deep burrows from where it emerges to feed on various forms of vegetation.

In 1863, South Australia took over control of the Northern Territory which, until then, had been administered by New South Wales. Needing contact with the north, South Australia constructed the Overland Telegraph Line which ran from Adelaide to Darwin, following the route of explorer McDouall Stuart, the first man to cross the continent from south to north. Huge cattle stations, many of which received water from artesian bores, were established. There was some mining, but the harsh conditions, isolation and exorbitant costs forced many of the mines to close. In 1911, the Commonwealth took control from South Australia, and Darwin was named capital of the Northern Territory.

In the early years, much of Australia's wealth and future lay on the backs of sheep. This growing and lucrative market attracted many men to the production of wool, Australia's first commodity to be exported. Flocks grew more numerous and more grazing areas were needed. Explorers, backed by Government, grazing and financial syndicates, trekked into the unknown in the hope of striking suitable pastures. Some were successful; others were thwarted by unbelievably difficult conditions. Droughts, floods and disease provoked further land hunting.

This radio telescope at Parkes in the central west of New South Wales, is used by the Radiophysics Department of the Commonwealth Scientific and Industrial Research Organisation, and began operating in 1961. A fertile wheat and sheep area, Parkes was once a gold-mining centre.

The red gum is found in all States except Tasmania. However, in some regions such as that around Greenough, Western Australia, the hot prevailing winds have left their mark.

In Van Diemen's Land, there was not enough grazing lands for the growing numbers of sheep. Across the Bass Strait small settlements had been established at Portland and Port Fairy, and the expedition of Hume and Hovell in 1824 to Port Phillip aroused considerable interest. A pastoral company, the Port Phillip Association, decided to ignore Government policy and utilise the suitable land that had been discovered. In May, 1835, John Batman, a syndicate member, landed at Port Phillip Bay. Eleven days later, he exchanged commodities with the local Aborigines for 600,000 acres of land. News spread quickly in Van Diemen's Land and many people were anxious to reap the riches of development. Another party, under the leadership of John Pascoe Fawkner, left Launceston to take up land, and overnight Melbourne sprang into existence. As the land was cleared and Aborigines driven from their homes, friction between the two races developed, and Captain William Lonsdale was sent to administer the settlement. In March 1837, Robert Hoddle arrived to survey the area. The system of free land grants had ended in 1831, and not regarding Batman's deed as legal, the Government began auctioning land. A 'boom' resulted and Melbourne grew.

Portable houses were imported from Sydney and Launceston. Pisa dwellings, wattle-and-daub huts and tents arose in haphazard order. The hard basalt proved

The cookhouse at the Brunette Downs, Northern Territory, picnic races.

difficult for masons, so limestone and bricks, along with all commodities, were imported at exorbitant rates. Banks, financed from England were established as immigrants poured into the thriving town. Land prices soared as speculators vied against each other at the Sydney auctions. Stock was pushed overland from New South Wales. Unsurveyed pastoral lands belonged to the Crown and were not for sale, so settlers just squatted and paid a licence fee of £10 annually plus a per-head-of-stock charge, and turned to the Commissioner of Crown Lands to settle arguments.

Wild speculation continued until the drought of 1838-40 brought a financial crash. The British withdrew their money from the highly capitalised wool industry which was then forced to slaughter sheep for tallow. Land prices fell and bankruptcies were common. In the towns, public work programmes were instigated while in the country only the fittest stock and men survived. In 1843, the New South Wales Legislative Council instigated a 'Liens of Wool and Mortgages on Stock' which allowed squatters to borrow on the security of the expected wool clip. Prices rose and with it prosperity. In 1847, the squatters were offered 14-year leases with option of house-paddock purchase. This led to property improvement and social inter-action. Craftsmen were imported, families and women brought out from England, fine homes established, and fences and outbuildings constructed. Growing flocks created the need for contractors for shearing, blacksmithing, horse breaking, and a host of other functions. Wool was being transported to markets by bullock teams, camel trains and paddle steamers, and land was continually being sought.

By 1845, most grazing land in Tasmania, Victoria, South Australia and New South Wales was occupied. In Queensland, Brisbane's isolated penal settlement had been closed after 15 years, surveyed and its blocks sold in Sydney. The fine grazing lands of the Darling Downs, discovered by Allan Cunningham in 1827, were being grazed by cattle. Men, driving their stock, moved into the unknown and squatted on vast sections of land for which they paid an annual licence fee of £10.

In May 1851, gold was discovered near Bathurst, New South Wales, and all hell broke loose. The gold rush had begun.

People left their towns, businesses, homes and families. Public works and building programmes stopped. Houses, churches and schools were abandoned. Labourers walked off the properties, leaving the squatters and their families to manage their vast properties as best they could. Melbourne, anxious to stop the mass exodus of people to New South Wales, was first to offer rewards for the discovery of payable goldfinds within its vicinity. Small towns did likewise and soon New South Wales and Victoria became dotted with goldfields.

Hunting with a woomera on Mornington Island, Queensland. This weapon provides more power and allows for greater accuracy.

Pelicans and water birds on Lake Menindee in western New South Wales.

The Tasman Bridge, which spans the Derwent River. Hobart nestles on the west side of the Derwent estuary, overlooked by Mount Wellington.

Catering for the national taste at Cairns, Northern Queensland.

In the shade of the baobab tree. Near Derby, Western Australia.

Pleasure craft clutter the Harbour. Here, Sydney's tourist highlights – the Opera House and the Harbour Bridge – are seen from a less familiar angle.

Thousands of canvas tents and bark huts stood among illegal 'grog' shanties. Water was often scarce and facilities non-existent. Most women and children remained in the cities. Because food, tools and clothes had to be transported by bullock drays, everything was expensive.

Australia was the first country in the world to form surf lifesaving clubs and to develop surf rescue techniques. The first beaches to be patrolled were Bronte and Waverley, Sydney, in 1894.

The snow-covered ski resort at Mount Buller, Victoria. In spring and summer the alpine area abounds in colourful wildflowers.

Large road trains ply the dusty Northern Territory roads to take the stock to market. Before trucks and trains were used, the animals had to be driven enormous distances in intense heat with little water or feed, and usually arrived at the abattoirs in poor condition.

Roads were made by the tramping feet of what seemed a never-ending stream of men. Conditions were often appalling as men, bearded and unwashed, and bothered by flies and mosquitoes, toiled in the dirt and dust of oppressive, and often dangerous mines during the hot summers and freezing winters. Floods and fires had to be endured, and long working hours often resulted in little reward. A large criminal element was attracted to the diggings and police were few and hard to recruit.

The diggers' grievances culminated in numerous clashes with authority — perhaps the best known occurring at the Eureka Stockade. Miners opposed the powers of land holders and demanded more representation. They refused to pay licence fees and objected to the ever increasing numbers of Chinese on the fields. This last objection ultimately resulted in the Immigration Restriction Bill passed by the Commonwealth Parliament in 1901.

Within three years of the gold rush, Australia's population had trebled. Many disillusioned goldseekers returned to the cities. When the gold petered out, many of the diggers turned towards the land for a living. Crown Land was quickly parcelled into lots. The squatters were allowed to purchase only a small portion of their holdings; the rest was to be sold at auction. Backed by the banks to which they were already in debt, squatters feverishly bought land. The small selector, inexperienced and with little money, found finance difficult, and was often forced to buy poor blocks. Many, finding the going tough, sold to the squatters they so hated with the result that most of the land ultimately landed back in the hands of the one-time squatters.

The Commercial Hotel at Moora, Western Australia.

Almost every Sunday for the past 20 years, a few of Rocky's friends have joined him at his 'tavern' near Longford, Tasmania, for a few beers and a chat. Rocky himself is in the foreground.

The Windsor Hotel in Melbourne is one of Australia's grandest.

Apart from the wealth brought to individuals and the country as a whole, the gold discoveries resulted in increased population, better communication systems, improved social and living standards.

In Queensland, the mining boom began in the 1860's and was followed in the 1890's by the discovery of huge mineral deposits in the arid areas of Western Australia, where even water had to be imported by camels at exorbitant costs. Where large amounts of gold were found, towns grew.

The years following the gold rush were prosperous. Mining companies were employing large numbers of men and making handsome profits. Large scale irrigation systems had opened up vast tracts of otherwise useless ground and farming was productive. There were developments in refrigeration, the propagation of crops suitable for drier land, better farming methods and cheaper transportation for goods produced. Markets for wool, wheat, dairy products, meat and sugar had been found overseas. Banks became more speculative and began buying and subdividing land.

'Grass trees' or 'Black Boys' on Cape Barren Island in Bass Strait.

An afternoon storm at Bundaberg, Queensland. Bundaberg is the centre of a sugar-cane growing area with most of its houses standing on tall stilts to capitalise on the cool breezes and remain above the swirling floodwaters when they occur.

The beautifully marked butterfly cod is a slow-swimming tropical fish with venomous spines along its back.

Sunset at Busselton on Geographe Bay near Cape Naturaliste, Western Australia. Busselton is the centre of a rich dairying area. The cape and the bay were named after his ships by the French explorer, Baudin, who explored the coast in 1801.

Mushroom Rock at Glen Innes, New South Wales. Years of erosion have exposed a towering pinnacle of balanced granite rocks.

One of many trees marked by the explorers Robert O'Hara Burke and William John Wills during their tragic overland journey from Melbourne to the Gulf of Carpentaria in 1860-1861.

Children play on a beach at Yirrkala on the eastern coast of Northern Territory.

The goanna is a meat-eating monitor lizard which can grow to a length of about two metres. There are a few varieties of goanna in Australia, and although they will generally avoid human contact, they can, if cornered, inflict a nasty bite.

The curved Stony Creek bridge forms part of the Kuranda-Cairns Railway which was completed in 1890.

Beside the Torrens River, Adelaide's Festival Hall was opened in June 1973, and provides the South Australian capital with an excellent forum for the arts.

Parrots at the Currumbin bird sanctuary on Queensland's Gold Coast. These 'wild' birds come twice daily to be fed. The sanctuary was founded in 1947 by Mr. A.M. Griffiths, and is now part of the National Trust.

It was a boom period for everyone until 1886 when the overseas price of wool fell dramatically. Suddenly there was no export market. Loans from abroad were withdrawn. Banks failed and bankruptcies were common. Unemployment was rife. It was a long depression. To alleviate the pressures, banks were brought under Government control and paper money instead of gold was used. Other countries reinvested in Australia, and after a long hard period, confidence returned and the world pressure eased.

The Governments again decided to resettle people on small farms. Estates, fallen during the depression, were bought by the Government and made available to groups of families at easy repayable rates. Some succeeded, but many left the land and returned to the growing cities.

Until 1823, the Governor of New South Wales had enormous powers vested in him by the British Government. Following this, a nominee Council presided over by the Governor, who still had power to veto any of its recommendations, was formed. Over the years the structure and formation of the Council changed and the

Darwin after Cyclone Tracey, and a warning to the light-fingered.

A property beside Lake George, New South Wales. Known as the 'disappearing lake', its water level rises and falls dramatically depending on the amount of silt washed into it by its many inflowing streams.

autocracy of the Governor was reduced. Each Colony wanted its own revenue and Crown Lands. The only argument appeared to be that of representation. Who, or what group of people should govern?

On 5th August, 1850, the Imperial Government made legal an Act allowing self-government to New South Wales, Victoria, South Australia and Tasmania. In 1859 Queensland became a separate Colony from New South Wales, and Western Australia followed suit in 1890.

Still under the aegis of the British Government, each Colony managed its own affairs, and for many years the need for Federation seemed pointless. Eventually, after

An old shingle-roof barn, Kempton, Tasmania.

The Great Barrier reef with Fairfax Island in the foreground and Musgrave Island. These islands form part of the Bunker Group.

The foundered hopes of early pioneers. Near Etadunna, South Australia.

skirmishes, threats and European occupation of the neighbouring Pacific islands, a constitution was drafted and accepted by all Colonies. The Act received Royal Assent on 9th July, 1900.

Modelled on the Westminster system of Government, and with a Governor-General to represent the Queen, the first Commonwealth Parliament opened in Melbourne on 9th May, 1901, and Edmund Barton became Australia's first Prime Minister. Papua, which had been governed by Queensland, came under Commonwealth control in 1906. Eight years later, Norfolk Island was also brought under Commonwealth protection.

Crater Lake in the Lake St Clair National Park, Tasmania, and a section of Cradle Mountain.

Fraser Island, separated from the Queensland coast near Maryborough by a narrow channel called Great Sandy Strait, is nearly 130 kilometres long and up to 22 kilometres wide. Made up of sand dunes which house stands of tall trees, fresh water lakes and numerous wildlife, it was named after Captain James Fraser who was killed by Aborigines after his ship the Stirling Castle was wrecked on its shore.

On the flat plain near Min Min, Queensland, the great road trains ride the unsealed roads. During the wet season these roads become impassable.

On the Murray River at Mildura, Victoria, the paddle steamers, Melbourne and the newly commissioned Avoca, move down the river towards the lock. In the 19th Century, paddle steamers played an important part in the development of the region.

Camels were introduced to Australia in 1840. Now, wild camels roam freely in Central Australia. They were used for exploration, the building of the Adelaide-Darwin Overland Telegraph Station, and survey work for the Trans-Australian Railway. They were highly regarded because of their suitability for desert conditions.

Isolated from the affairs of most of the world, yet still very much under the influence of Great Britain, Australia prospered, the major source of its wealth being in primary industries. When World War I broke out in 1914, Britain called on Australia for support.

Volunteers, most of whom were excellent bushmen, hastily enrolled. Industry was converted to produce the goods necessary to equip the departing troops. What was not available, or could not be quickly procured, was improvised. With thousands of men, equipment, horses and food to transport, the Government bought and requisitioned ships. To finance the war machine, loans were acquired and the Government once again used paper money, only a quarter of which was backed by gold. Australia's losses were heavy. Of a population of under five million, over 60,000 men were killed and over 100,000 wounded.

After the war, returning servicemen were encouraged to settle on the land, but through inexperience and hardship, and astronomical costs, this was not a success. Housing was short and assimilation problems were enormous. Large amounts of money were borrowed from overseas.

Compared to the war years, the 1920's were good, but like the depression of the 1890's, prices on world markets fell and the 1930's brought lean times. No sooner had the country begun to recover than Hitler invaded Poland and Great Britain declared war on Germany. Once again Australia mobilised. This time the war involved a more direct threat to Australia's security with the Japanese occupation of the islands to the north. For the first time in its history, bombs fell on Australian soil with the Japanese air raids on Darwin in 1942. The same year, two Japanese midget submarines broke through the defences of Sydney Harbour.

Since the war, there has been an enormous influx of immigrants to Australia, bringing with them radical changes in the country's outlook, and a deeper awareness of other life-styles and cultural aspirations.

Australia is a great land in more ways than one. It is unique, an experience, a state of mind. It signifies challenge and hope, where every man can forge the dreams of his own destiny under the guiding symbol of the Southern Cross.